HOW TO DRAW VAMPIRES,
ZOMBIES, AND OTHER MONSTERS

Mark Bergin

PowerKiDS press™

New York

Published in 2012 by The Rosen Publishing Group, Inc.
29 East 21st Street, New York, NY 10010

Editor: Rob Walker
U.S. Editor: Kara Murray

Library of Congress Cataloging-in-Publication Data

Bergin, Mark.
 How to draw vampires, zombies, and other monsters / by Mark Bergin. — 1st ed.
     p. cm. — (How to draw)
 Includes index.
  ISBN 978-1-4488-4512-5 (library binding) —
 ISBN 978-1-4488-4524-8 (pbk.) —
 ISBN 978-1-4488-4525-5 (6-pack)
 1. Vampires in art—Juvenile literature.
 2. Monsters in art—Juvenile literature.
 3. Drawing—Technique—Juvenile literature. I. Title.
  NC825.V36B47 2012
 743'.87—dc22

                          2010049195

Manufactured in China

CPSIA Compliance Information: Batch #SS1102PK: For Further Information contact
Rosen Publishing, New York, New York at 1-800-237-9932

PAPER FROM
SUSTAINABLE
FORESTS

Contents

Making a Start

Learning to draw is about looking and seeing. Keep practicing and get to know your subject. Use a sketchbook to make quick drawings. Start by doodling and experimenting with shapes and patterns. There are many ways to draw, but this book shows only some methods. Visit art galleries, look at artists' drawings, and see how your friends draw, but above all, find your own way.

You can practice drawing figures using an artist's model. This is a small wooden figure that can be put into various poses.

When drawing from photos, use construction lines to help you understand the form of the body and how each of its parts relate to each other.

Practice sketching people in everyday surroundings. This will help you draw faster and train you to quickly capture the main elements of a pose.

Try sketching friends and family in creepy poses at home.

Perspective

If you look at a figure from different viewpoints, you will see that whichever part is closest to you looks larger, and the part farthest away from you looks smallest. Drawing in perspective is a way of creating a feeling of depth, or of suggesting three dimensions on a flat surface.

The vanishing point (V.P.) is the place in a perspective drawing where parallel lines appear to meet. The position of the vanishing point depends on the viewer's eye level.

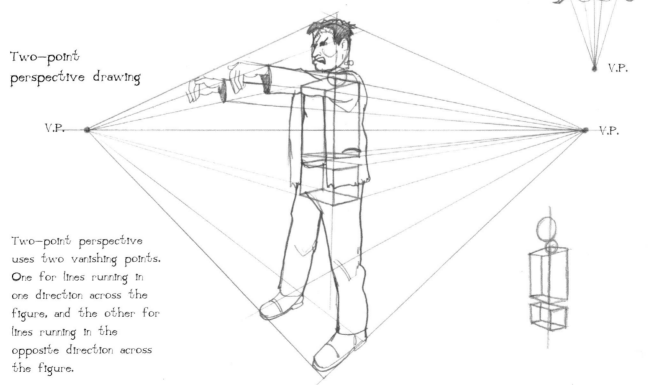

Two–point perspective drawing

V.P.

V.P.

V.P.

Two–point perspective uses two vanishing points. One for lines running in one direction across the figure, and the other for lines running in the opposite direction across the figure.

Three-point perspective drawing

Three-point perspective drawings use three vanishing points. This method is good for drawing a figure from a more dramatic angle.

V.P.

V.P.

V.P.

V.P.

V.P.

V.P.

V.P. = vanishing point

7

Drawing Materials

Try using different types of drawing papers and materials. Experiment with charcoal, wax crayons, and pastels. All pens, from felt-tips to ballpoints, will make interesting marks. Try drawing with pen and ink on wet paper for a variety of results.

Silhouette is a style of drawing that uses only a solid black shape.

Ink

Felt-tip

Charcoal is very soft and can be used for big, bold drawings. Ask an adult to spray your charcoal drawings with fixative to prevent smudging.

You can create special effects in a drawing done with **wax crayons** by scraping parts of the color away.

8

Pencil

Hard **pencil** leads are grayer and soft pencil leads are blacker. Hard pencils are graded from #2½ to #4 (the hardest). A #1 pencil is a soft pencil.

Pastels are even softer than charcoal and come in a wide range of colors. Ask an adult to spray your pastel drawings with fixative to prevent smudging.

Ink

Lines drawn in ink cannot be erased, so keep your ink drawings sketchy and less rigid. Do not worry about mistakes as these lines can be lost in the drawing as it develops.

Creating Characters

Creating a scary character can be a lot of fun. Different characters and features can all be created from the same basic starting point.

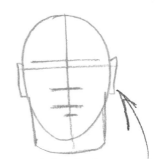

Basic head construction.

Draw an oval head shape and mark in the position of facial features with construction lines.

Frankenstein's monster

Male vampire

Devil

Grim Reaper

Zombie

Witch

Female vampire

Ghost

Try to see how many different characters you can create from your imagination.

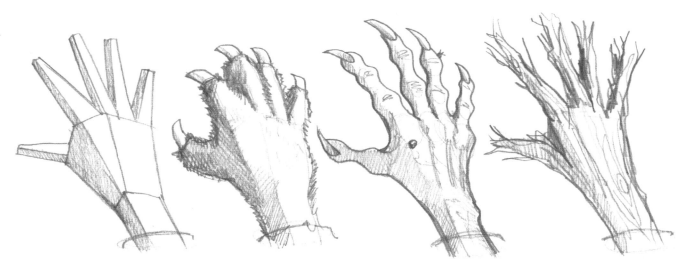

Draw a basic hand shape with straight construction lines.

Here are a few examples of how scary monster hands can be created from the first template.

Accessories

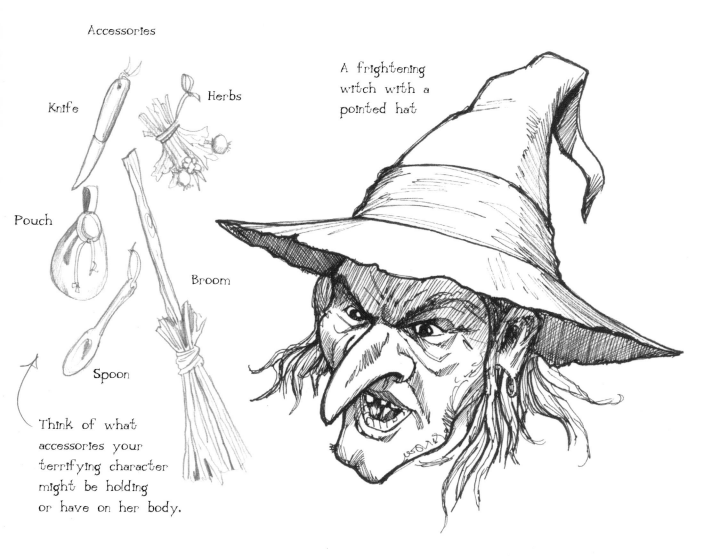

Knife

Herbs

Pouch

Broom

Spoon

A frightening witch with a pointed hat

Think of what accessories your terrifying character might be holding or have on her body.

Drawing Movement

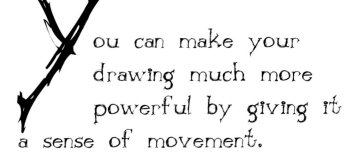

Y ou can make your drawing much more powerful by giving it a sense of movement.

Start by drawing stick figures in action poses.

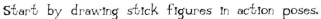

These can be the basis of your drawing showing where each limb is according to the position of the body.

A jumping ghoul

This ghoul is midjump. You can see how this pose is developed from the stick figure shown.

This finished drawing gives a sense of action. Adding movement lines around the drawing gives it a sense of momentum. The horse's mane and tail also fly out behind it as do the billowing clothes of the Grim Reaper.

Vampire

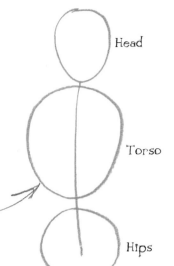

Vampires are said to prowl the night in search of unsuspecting victims to plunge their teeth into and suck their blood dry.

Draw a circle for the head and two ovals for the torso and hips.

Head

Torso

Hips

Add construction lines to the face to position the facial features.

Draw the figure's arms with straight lines, adding small circles for the joints.

Add ovals for the hands.

Add the legs with long, straight lines and small circles for the joints.

Sketch in the shape of the feet. There are a triangle and an oval.

Draw a simple candle in the vampire's hand.

Sketch in the facial features using the construction lines as a guide. Add the V-shaped hairline.

Add fingers to the oval hand.

Sketch in the shirt, adding cuffs and collar.

Draw the cape and collar using flowing, curved lines.

Add the vest and pants with simple lines.

Complete the details of the face. Add tone to the hair and the mouth.

Draw the chain using circles.

Add details to the candle and hands.

Add shading to areas light would not reach.

Add buttons and details to the vest.

Draw long, curved lines for folds in the cape.

Finish the detail on the shoes.

Use an eraser to remove any unwanted construction lines.

15

Zombie

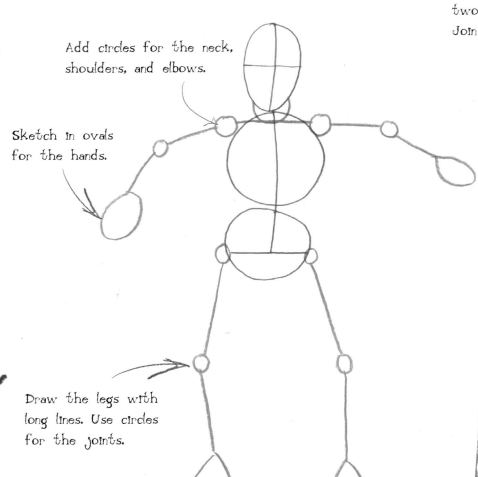

These dead people are said to have risen and are walking the earth! The zombies will not stop until they have killed you and made you like them.

Sketch in basic construction lines to place facial features.

Head

Torso

Hips

Draw an oval for the head and two circles for the torso and hips. Join these with a center line.

Add circles for the neck, shoulders, and elbows.

Sketch in ovals for the hands.

Draw the legs with long lines. Use circles for the joints.

Light from above

Light from a diagonal angle from above

Light from the side

Light from below

Light

Changing the direction of the light source in a drawing can create drama and mood.

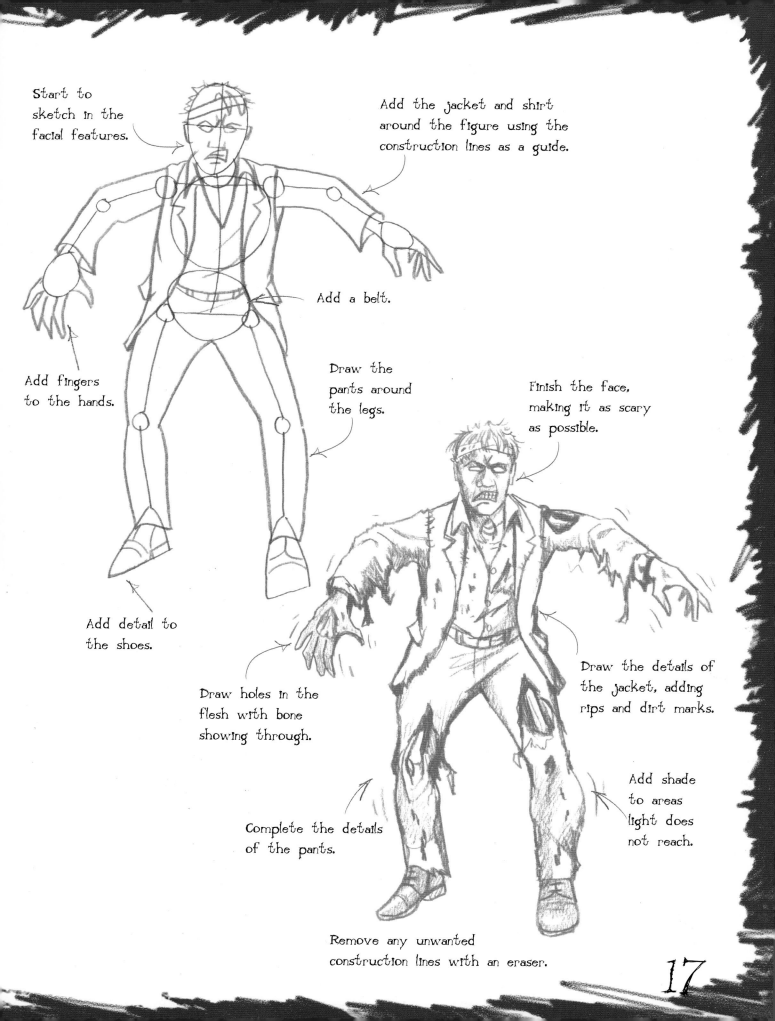

Start to
sketch in the
facial features.

Add the jacket and shirt
around the figure using the
construction lines as a guide.

Add a belt.

Add fingers
to the hands.

Draw the
pants around
the legs.

Finish the face,
making it as scary
as possible.

Add detail to
the shoes.

Draw holes in the
flesh with bone
showing through.

Draw the details of
the jacket, adding
rips and dirt marks.

Add shade
to areas
light does
not reach.

Complete the details
of the pants.

Remove any unwanted
construction lines with an eraser.

17

Ghoul

Ghouls are thought to haunt graveyards or any other place that dead human flesh can be found. They devour the rotting meat, leaving nothing but the bones.

Draw a long oval for the head.

Head

Torso

Draw circles for the torso and hips.

Draw a curved line for the bent spine.

Add construction lines to the head to place the facial features.

Position the arms using lines and circles for the joints.

Sketch in ovals for the hands.

Add long lines for the legs and circles for the joints.

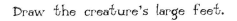

Draw the creature's large feet.

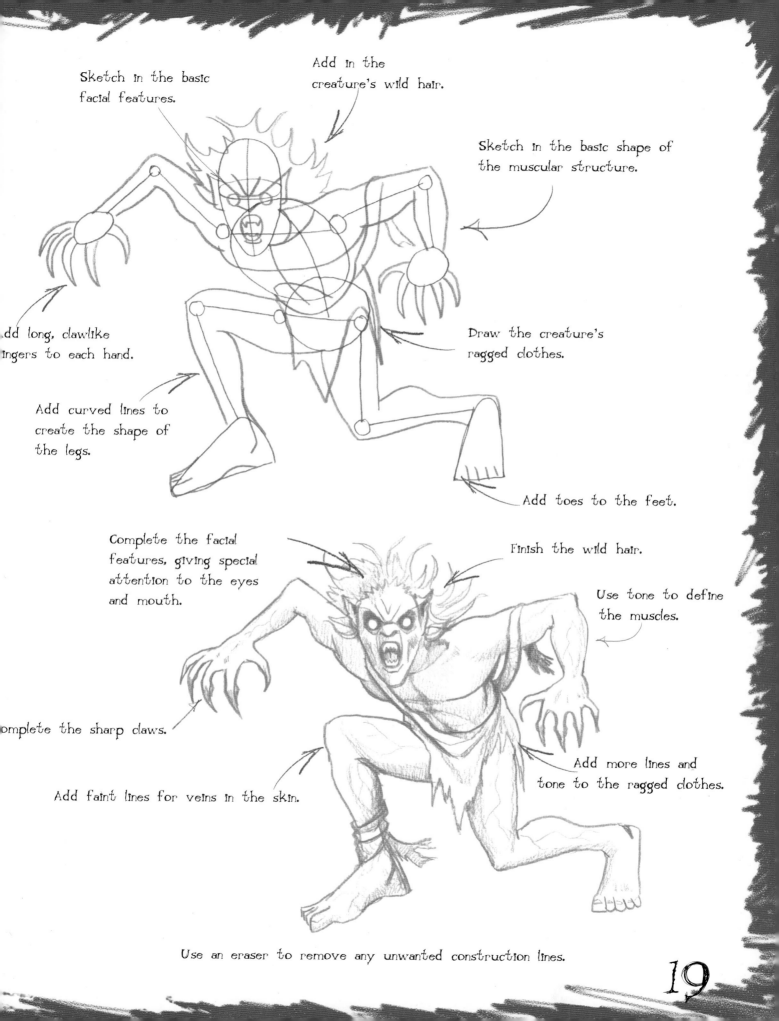

Sketch in the basic facial features.

Add in the creature's wild hair.

Sketch in the basic shape of the muscular structure.

dd long, clawlike ingers to each hand.

Add curved lines to create the shape of the legs.

Draw the creature's ragged clothes.

Add toes to the feet.

Complete the facial features, giving special attention to the eyes and mouth.

Finish the wild hair.

Use tone to define the muscles.

omplete the sharp claws.

Add faint lines for veins in the skin.

Add more lines and tone to the ragged clothes.

Use an eraser to remove any unwanted construction lines.

19

Werewolf

Beware the full moon! Once this lunar phase is entered, these cursed people are said to transform into creatures that are half man and half wolf and will tear their victims apart!

Head

Torso

Hips

Sketch an oval for the head and two circles for the torso and hips. Add a center line for the spine and a line for the hips.

Add lines for the arms with circles for the joints.

Add circles for the hands.

Draw short lines for the legs.

Draw circles to indicate joints.

Add two large, flipperlike feet.

Position the ear and eye.

Sketch in construction lines for the shape of the snout.

Add claws to the hands.

Join the head to the shoulders.

Finish the snout details and add sharp teeth.

Sketch on the ripped pants.

Draw lots of short lines to indicate the fur.

Join the torso to the hips.

Draw the limbs using the construction lines as a guide.

Add the shape of the tail.

Complete the hands, adding pads and claws.

Add claws to the feet.

Finish the furry tail.

Complete the torn and ragged pants.

Remove any unwanted construction lines with an eraser.

Draw the details of the elongated feet.

Ghost

Ghosts are thought to be the souls of dead people who cannot rest. They haunt the living at night, filling them with terror.

Head

Torso

Hips

Sketch three ovals for the head, torso, and hips. Join these with a center line for the spine.

Sketch a construction line to place the eyes.

Add lines for the arms, with circles for the joints.

Add ovals for the hands.

Add long lines for the legs with circles for the joints.

Sketch in basic shapes for the feet.

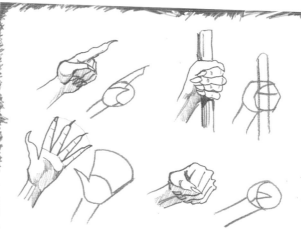

Drawing Hands

Practice sketching your own hands in different positions. This will help you draw characters with expressive hands.

Add pointed fingers.

Sketch in the arms using the construction lines as a guide.

Draw dark holes for the eyes, nostrils, and mouth.

Sketch in curved lines for the shape of the chest.

Add the outline of the body with long, curved lines.

Add long, wavy lines for the hair.

Draw lines to show the dress fabric hanging loosely on the figure.

Draw the legs using the construction lines as a guide.

Shade areas where light would not reach.

Add straggly lines to create the ragged sleeves and hemline.

Remove any unwanted construction lines.

Draw the toes.

23

Witch

T he grotesque appearance of this menacing and sly old crone is only matched by her cruelty and magical powers.

Add a construction line to place the eyes.

Head

Torso

Hips

Sketch in the basic body shapes with three ovals. Connect these by drawing a line for the spine.

Sketch in a line to show the direction the head faces.

Draw lines for the arms, with circles for the joints.

Add ovals for hands.

Add a long, straight line for the witch's broom.

Draw long lines for the legs, with circles for the joints.

Add triangular shapes for the feet.

Draw the arms using the construction lines as a guide.

Draw the shape of the witch's crooked hat.

Add basic facial features, including a long nose!

Draw this hand grasping the broom.

Draw long, flaring lines for the clothes.

Add the shape of the broom bristles.

Complete the details and shading of the crooked hat.

Add ragged edges to her sleeves and clothes.

Finish the ugly facial features.

Draw sharp lines for magic shooting out of the witch's hand.

Add shading to areas where light will not reach.

Add trinkets to the witch's belt.

Add tears and holes to the clothing.

Using an eraser, remove any unwanted construction lines.

Frankenstein's Monster

Victor Frankenstein seized body parts to create a living being in a terrifying electrical experiment. This manmade creature walks the night alone.

Head

Draw the position of the eyes.

Torso

Hips

Draw two ovals for the head and torso and a circle for the hips. Draw a center line and a horizontal line for the hips.

Add lines to draw outstretched arms through the torso. Draw circles for the joints.

Add ovals for the hands.

Action Poses

Draw lots of small stick figures to find the best pose. Try posing in front of a mirror to figure out what looks best.

Draw long lines for the legs, with circles for the joints.

Sketch in two triangular shapes for the feet.

Draw fingers on the hands.

Add basic facial features.

Sketch in the hair.

Add a bolt through the neck.

Sketch in the basic shape of the jacket. Make the sleeves look short.

Add a pocket to the jacket.

Draw the pants and belt using the construction lines as a guide.

Finish the details of the head.

Add some details to the shoes.

Add shading to areas where light will not reach.

Draw patches on the knee and elbow.

Draw the laces and extra detail on the shoes.

Use an eraser to remove any unwanted construction lines.

Scarecrow

This frightening character bursts into life on Halloween, scaring bystanders and terrorizing nearby towns.

Head

Torso

Hips

Draw two circles for the head and hips and an oval for the torso. Add a curved line for the spine and a horizontal line at the hips.

Draw straight lines for the arms, with circles for the joints.

Add ovals for the hands.

Add long lines for the legs, with circles for the joints.

Add triangles for the feet.

Draw the shape of the pumpkin head. Add its scary features.

Draw the branchlike shapes for the fingers.

Add the shape of the scarf.

Draw the ragged shape of the coat using the construction lines as a guide.

Draw a drawstring belt.

Add details to the coat, like tears and patches.

Draw the feet as spiky branch shapes.

Complete the spiky, branchlike hands.

Add shading to areas where light will not reach.

Use jagged lines for the ragged sleeves, pants, and hemlines.

Remove any unwanted construction lines with an eraser.

The Grim Reaper

Hope you do not meet up with this cloaked figure anytime soon! His appearance is said to mean your life has come to an end, as he has come to collect your soul.

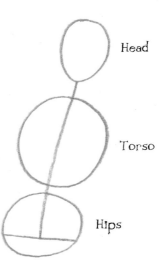

Head

Torso

Hips

Draw rounded shapes for the head, neck, torso, and hips. Add a line for the spine.

Sketch in the construction lines for the facial features.

Draw a long, curved line for the scythe.

Draw straight lines for the arms, with circles for the joints.

Add ovals for the hands.

Sketch in long lines for the legs, with circles for the joints.

Sketch in the shapes of the feet.

Draw the basic skull features.

Draw the shape of the head inside a loose-fitting hood.

Add the long, open sleeves of the cloak.

Add curved lines for the blade.

Sketch in bony fingers holding the scythe.

Add jagged lines for the flowing edges of the cape and the hemline.

Finish the skull details.

Add lines to create the bony feet.

Complete the details of the scythe.

Add shading to areas where light would not reach.

Draw a pile of skulls and bones.

Add tonal lines for folds in the cloak.

Use an eraser to remove any unwanted construction lines.

Glossary

center line (SEN–tur LYN) Often used as the starting point of the drawing, it marks the middle of the object or figure.

construction lines (kun–STRUK–shun LYNZ) Guidelines used in the early stages of a drawing and usually erased later.

fixative (FIK–suh–tiv) A type of resin that is sprayed over a finished drawing to prevent smudging. It should be used only by an adult.

perspective (per–SPEK–tiv) A method of drawing in which near objects are shown larger than faraway objects to give an impression of depth.

Pose (POHZ) The position assumed by a figure.

silhouette (sih–luh–WET) A drawing that shows only a flat, dark shape, like a shadow.

sketchbook (SKECH–buhk) A book in which quick drawings are made.

vanishing point (VA–nish–ing POYNT) The place in a perspective drawing where parallel lines appear to meet.

Index

Web Sites

Due to the changing nature of Internet links, PowerKids Press has developed an online list of Web sites related to the subject of this book. This site is updated regularly. Please use this link to access the list:

www.powerkidslinks.com/htd/vampires/